CONTAGIOUS LEADERSHIP

DONTE' HILL

Contagious Leadership
Donte' Hill
pp. 100

For information, contact:
Donte' Hill
4320 Deerwood Lake Parkway, Suite 101-253
Jacksonville, FL 32216
(229) 860-0816
Website: www.kcsportsconsulting.com

ISBN 13: 978-1466470224
ISBN 10: 1466470224

Printed in the United States of America

TABLE OF CONTENTS

DEDICATION

I dedicate this book to the most contagious person I know; who gave me the blueprint for being contagious; who encouraged me to have friends of every shape, size, color, and denomination; and who reminds me that it's about what is on the inside of a person that counts.
This is for my mother Bonitha Hill-Haggerty; I love you!

ADVANCE PRAISE
FOR CONTAGIOUS LEADERSHIP

"Revolutionary and Inspiring! Whether you are a new college graduate, entrepreneur or executive, Contagious Leadership is a must Read."

> – Michael Calloway, Chik-Fil-A at Western Hills
> Owner/Operator

"Contagious Leadership will help you understand that while success might be easier said than done, focusing on a few fundamentals will dramatically increase your probability of success and help you have fun doing it."

> – Teresa Brown, Baymeadows Charter School
> Principal and Former University of Florida
> Women's Basketball Player

Making contagious team members is the competitive edge today. This book can jump-start you in that direction."

> – Tara Wallach, University of Michigan
> Director of Softball Operations

"Contagious Leadership moves us to define who we are in a new and illuminating way! Contagious Leadership is a guidebook for the leaders of the future. Thank you, Donte'!"

> – Ira Childress, NCAA
> Assistant Director of Leadership Development

"Whether you're trying to move yourself forward or coaching others to achieve greatness, this book shows you how to tap into hidden potential and unleash the passion and skills you need to succeed. Contagious Leadership is a counter intuitive, practical, and inspiring book that will change the way you think about performance."

– Josh Kutchinski, Mesa Community College
Assistant Athletic Director/Student Success Coordinator

"Donte' is bringing a fresh and bold perspective to how great Leaders impact others in his new book Contagious Leadership! All emerging stars must read this!"

– Shawn Williams, YMCA Indianapolis
Assistant Program Coordinator

"Contagious Leadership has never been more important. For anyone wanting to be a better leader, every page of Donte's book offers practical advice."

– Melissa Adams, Blue Cross Blue Shield of Florida
Senior Management of New Media

"Donte' provides a powerful message to all who lead people, one that will produce exceptional loyalty and results. These principles can make a huge difference."

– Lillian McNeil, Verizon Wireless
Senior Sales Trainer

"Deep and meaningful connections with people in business can change the path of your career. This is a brilliant playbook for professionals who want to step up their game and truly own their success."

– Bill Houston NFL Jacksonville Jaguars
Senior Account Executive

FOREWARD

The word contagious is generally referred to in the negative form. It is used to describe a disease or virus. Something that is contagious suggests that it has the ability to be caught, replicated, and/or reproduced, and not necessarily by invitation.

Leadership – simply defined as; "being worthy to follow" has resulted in countless volumes of books– many of which have become best sellers. Due to the sheer volume of interest and following of the topic, there is evidence that there is room for more exploration and discussion on how leadership can be accomplished.

The view points in Donte' Hill's book entitled 'Contagious Leadership' has done just that. It has pushed the boundaries of the typical definition of leadership and has exposed a new way of leading others.

Donte' has skillfully taken the negative definition of 'contagious' and linked it with 'leadership,' to create a new and evolving way to lead others. These two words join to promote action, represent meaning, evoke thoughtfulness, and exude intent.

The unique approach taken in this book is that 'without invitation' the principles, methodologies, and practices will overtake the followers when led by the leadership principles.

In fact, the more I read Donte's book, it is clear that being 'contagious' is not about 'taking over' but in the positive, is about being a magnet – drawing one into; becoming a leader.

Contagious Leadership reminds the leader that it doesn't matter what prestigious MBA school you went to, or how much money you make, or what color your skin is, everyone has the ability to be an effective leader. The practical applications available at the end of each chapter compel the leader to engage in their personal leadership style. Navigating through the chapters provides life changing benefits.

Contagious Leadership is given to you so that you can share with others! Become a new leader and mold our future leaders with the blessing that God has given in Contagious Leadership!

Glenn Henderson – Author, Founder and Host of "Rock Solid Principles"

INTRODUCTION

Enriching your organization with multiple leaders will help make your job more manageable, create a more effective working environment, and will keep retention at an all time low. Not only is the growth of your organization important, but also so is the growth and development of your team and employees.

Leadership is a hot topic among sport organizations, businesses, religious practices, and politics. Everyday an internet search is done by someone in the world looking for more information on leadership. Sometimes the search is for leadership quotes to inspire themselves or someone else, other times it is a search on leadership traits and qualities, but often times it is a search on leadership development; how to become a better and more productive leader and how to develop others. There is so much information out there that it can become overwhelming and confusing on how to begin developing leadership abilities and attitudes of individuals. Have no fear, Contagious Leadership brings it all to you in a nice and simplistic package.

Everyone can develop his or her leadership effectiveness. To achieve and develop better leadership traits, it takes focus, practice, and persistence more akin to learning a musical instrument than reading a book. What we outline hear are some practical steps for you to be an outstanding leader in your environment. A few key concepts that I touch on are integration and effective coaching, goal setting, self-efficacy, vision, and succession planning.

Changing the way you interact with your employees and team managers is going to be uncomfortable, but trust that in the long run that your organization will be in a better and more profitable place. Your new philosophy that you are adapting to, will not only challenge yourself but it will also challenge others. Empowering your people to strengthen their leadership skills will birth an intrinsic motivation within them and they will strive to succeed for you, themselves, and for the team.

When I thought about writing this book I thought about what it means to be contagious; transferable, infectious, and the ability to spread from person to person. Like a smile or laughter can change a mood, effective leadership can rapidly change the culture and values of an organization. In my experience, I have been fortunate enough to develop leaders that have impacted their organizations and directly influenced those around them. Witnessing this first hand sparked a flame within me to want to help others become successful leaders. It is my goal to be contagious and spread my philosophy of success to you and leaders of tomorrow, so that you can then go out and be contagious to others.

Have you ever been around someone with a cold? You were conscious of how close you got to them to avoid catching that cold. The key was trying to stay away from their germs so you would not be infected. Contagious Leadership is designed so that your organization is so close to you that they become infected with your vision, enthusiasm, and thirst for greatness. My hope for this book is that you will understand and practice the leadership skills that I have provided to you; realizing that regardless of your strengths and weaknesses you are not immune from leadership. I want your organization to become so infected with your leadership that you are the go-to guru of personal development, and are also making major changes in your organization. Doesn't this sound exciting to you? It was sure exciting putting this together, so let's start becoming contagious!

I

SHARING THE ROLES

CHAPTER 1
CRAFTING A SHARED PURPOSE

"The way you get meaning into your life is to devote yourself to loving others, devote yourself to your community around you, and devote yourself to creating something that gives you purpose and meaning."

-Mitch Albom

Sharing the purpose of your organization is the first place to start when looking to gain credibility, camaraderie, and confidence in your team. The purpose of an organization is much larger than goals and specific outcomes. It's about the overall culture, the atmosphere that you create for your team, and how your public sees you. The University of Michigan is a public institution dedicated to offering "an uncommon education for the common man."[1] This statement is their ultimate purpose. By providing state of the art technology, top notch professors, fully equipped athletic facilities, museums and access to a robust art community, and hundreds of areas of study, the university has made itself a world-class, highly prestigious university. To accomplish all that they have, the university had to set hundreds of small and large goals, but the heart of their movement; what drove them to success started with their vision of providing "an uncommon education for the common man," and having employees who believed in the same purpose.

Sharing the purpose creates enthusiastic teammates that believe they are involved in the growth and outcome of the organization. Have you ever sat in a company's new employee orientation and watched the faces of the new hires as the company leaders explain their purpose and future goals for the company? What you will notice is that the new employees are excited, they are smiling, and you can tell they are ready to get to work. It is that initial moment when they have bought into what your purpose is. Now your job is to ensure that they still believe three months, six months, and two years later, as well as when they leave for their retirement.

You don't have to be a brand new team or company to create a purpose. Depending on the level of management a leader is entering into they have a few different options.

A) They could create or suggest creating a brand new purpose for the organization,

B) They could keep the original purpose but tweak the goals that follow the purpose, or

C) They can do nothing.

---

[1] University of Michigan Vision Statement. www.umich.edu/pres/mission

Which option do you think would be best if you were the new leader of an organization?

You should have trouble answering this question because without further information there is no correct answer. Each position that you take on will require a survey of the company. It is important to understanding where the company wants to go, what plans they have to get there, how well they are doing to reach that ultimate purpose, and how your position impacts the outcome. It is very important to know and understand the history of the organization before you start making changes. Once you understand the interworking and movement of the company you can then begin assessing how you will proceed. Regardless of which option you choose, as a leader you need to create a strategic plan that lays out a timeline of short and long term goals for the company as a whole and for each department. This plan does not have to be shiny and new, it can be an updated version of what is already in place. What is important is that you share it with your investors, employees and/or team so that they understand where you want the company to go and so that everyone involved is on the same page. The more direction you give and the clearer and precise your purpose is, the more likely your employers will buy in. Be forewarned that not everyone may buy in, and that's ok...all this could mean is that they are not in the right organization or on the right team that fits them best. For those that do buy in though, you will have a team that is willing to go the extra mile.

Mike Krzyzewski, the basketball coach at Duke University, has been one of the most successful college basketball coaches of all time. His coaching style is in part a demonstration of his experiences as a player and later as a coach under Bobby Knight, the basketball coach at Indiana and former coach of Army. Although Mike Krzyzewski shares Bobby Knight's obsession and dedication to winning, Krzyzewski takes a different route from his mentor in his methodology of achieving that success. Unlike Knight, Coach K exercises a more endearing and nurturing coaching philosophy. His dedication to his players extends beyond the basketball court and beyond their college experience, which is proven by the countless endorsements from both current and former athletes. Although no one simple leadership style can properly define Coach K's coaching philosophy, one advanced leadership style by Robert House can expose some of his secrets. Robert House suggests that an effective leader is one who clarifies paths through which followers can achieve both task-oriented and personal goals[2]. The primary focus of this style involves setting and achieving the highest level goals attainable at any particular discipline. In the case of college basketball, there is arguably no other finer achievement than winning the NCAA National Championship.

The same concept applies to business. As a leader you need to clearly define the purpose and clarify specific paths that your employees can follow to become better at their own business and make your business better. If your team believes in your purpose and believes you have an interest in their professional and personal goals, you can bet they will run through walls for you. Well maybe not walls, but they will have the organization's best interest at heart. If everyone has the best intentions for the organization, they work harder, they work more efficiently, and they work to win.

Once the paths are laid out and everyone involved is on board, you then can focus on each person's purpose on the team and identify their strengths and weaknesses. Referring back to Mike Krzyzewski, he indicates a team is like a fist and a fist doesn't function well unless all fingers are working together as a unit. No one finger or in the team concept, player is more important than the whole. Your company is the fist and each finger is a department. One department is not more important than the other, but each has its own strengths and depends on one another to achieve success. As a leader it is important for you and your management team to outline each department's role and identify the strengths and weaknesses of each person in that department to understand how they will impact the bottom line. From there you organize your department's interior so that team members can build off of each other's talents and skills.

The last piece of sharing the vision is to hold your team accountable. You have laid the ground work of where the organization is going and how you are going to get there, now it's time to put the plan in action. If everyone is on board, holding them accountable will be a piece of cake because you won't have to. If done correctly, your team will hold each other accountable. They will be there to help each other through struggles; they will encourage

---

[2] Robert J.House,"A Path-Goal Theory of Leader Effectiveness," Administrative Science Quarterly(September 1971), pp.321–328; and House and Terence R.Mitchell, "Path-Goal Theory of Leadership," Journal of Contemporary Business(Autumn 1974), pp.81–97.

each other, celebrate each other's successes, and will call team members out when someone isn't pulling their weight.

Keep in mind that the main word is "shared" not "sell" purpose. Selling entails being persuasive and maintaining a high relationship between the manager and their employee. Instead you are motivating your team and asking them to have passion in the organization. Although you have to direct your team of employees to a certain extent, you do not do it in a manner as to produce a low-relationship style. Take an interest in your employees and continually remind them of how their input, talents, and skills help move the company closer towards the main purpose.

CRAFTING A SHARED PURPOSE

1. What is your organizations ultimate purpose of business?

2. What is your organization's mission statement?
    a. Does everyone buy into it?
    b. If not, why don't they?

3. What are some short and long term goals of your organization?
    a. Of your department?

4. What is the passion level in your group/organization?

5. Is your team enthusiastic about the group's purpose?

6. What is your leadership style?
    a. Why did you develop this style of leadership?
    b. Is this style working?
    c. How or why is it not?
    d. How can you improve it?

7. If motivation is low on your team, how could you create more enthusiasm?

8. If motivation is high, what can you do to keep it at this level?

9. What other company wide issues are your organization struggling with?

CHAPTER 2
DEVELOPING A SHARED VISION

*"If you don't care where you are going,
then it doesn't matter which way you go."*

-Lewis Carroll

CHAPTER 2: DEVELOPING A SHARED VISION

In the Disney cartoon classic Alice in Wonderland, Alice asks the Cheshire cat to tell her which way to go, and he responds that it depends on where you would like to go. When Alice replies that it doesn't matter, the cat responds with "then it doesn't matter which way you go." This scenario speaks volumes about the importance of creating a shared vision. It is reflective of the shortsighted focus that is all too common in organizations today. [3] Without a shared vision, it is entirely too easy to go off path.

Shared vision focuses on the realm of group process, converting the company into 'our company'. Creating momentum, collaboration, and energy in a group is tremendously important according to Peter Senge, American scientist and director of the Center for Organizational Learning at MIT. It creates a sense of commonality and gives coherence to diverse activities. To accomplish these results everyone involved needs to feel inspired and understand the direction in which they are moving.[4]

A shared vision is much more than a list of goals. It needs to be something that inspires people and gets them to pull together for cooperative action. When people understand what the group is trying to accomplish and buy into it, they really get energized. Encourage each of your team members to articulate and shape desires and expectations for a specific project, their specific department, and the organization as a whole. When each individual express themselves, they create a culture that values the full and effective participation of all of its members, regardless of personal identity, experience, or background. What you ideally want is for people to be able to see that they are adding a contribution and are personally involved in bringing the vision to life. This is the "shared" aspect of the vision.

To create a collaborative environment you need to be a leader that encourages openness, dissolves team and office politics, and listens to the team. The best way to lead people into the future is to connect with them deeply in the present. To create shared visions you have to listen very, very closely to others, appreciate their hopes, and attend to their needs. The best leaders are able to bring their team into the future because they engage in the oldest form of research: They observe the human condition.

---

[3] http://ezinearticles.com/?expert=Marty_Jacobs
[4] http://www.infed.org/thinkers/senge.htm

On November 4, 2009 the New York Yankees won their 27th World Series. With more championships than any other franchise in North American professional sports history, and throughout their existence, to have some of the most celebrated players in the Major League, it's no wonder they have an obsessed following of fans. Fans follow the Yankees because they are winners, they exude confidence, and they have exceptional leadership, and it is consistent throughout the organization. It is very present that there is a shared vision hard at work, and from what I can tell there are four key pieces that make up this shared vision for the New York Yankees Organization.

Passion – The New York Yankees have a passion for the game of baseball and for their own teammates. This love for the game and their baseball family can be seen on their faces, in their enthusiasm and in the fun that they have on the field day in and day out. They set high bars for themselves and meet every challenge together as one. Their leader Joe Girardi shared a clear vision by choosing the #27 and wearing it boldly on his back for everyone to see the clear common goal – win the Yankees' 27th World Series. Thus, within two years their goal was reached.

Development – Collectively, the team sets individual and team goals. Each person knows each other's goals and they hold each other accountable. It is important to the Yankees that parts of their goals are focused on self-improvement. In 2008 Derek Jeter had what some would call a slump, but he persevered and worked hard and was able to up his own performance the following year. Alex Rodriguez is another example of personal growth, he started out as one of the most psychologically weak members on the team and is now seen as a complete player – mentally, physically, and emotionally solid. Transformation and self-improvement is not only meant for the power hitters, it is also encouraged for the young players. The Yankees give their green players every opportunity to develop by sending them back to the farm team, working with the coaches and then finally giving them the chance to contribute…look at Robinson Cano.

Diversity and Inclusion – With players from Panama, Venezuela, Japan, Mexico, Puerto Rico, and America, the Yankees team is highly diverse. The team is an example of how differences are embraced and used to an advantage. They accept one another, understand each other's strengths and weaknesses, and use their unique experiences to build a strong and winning team.

Communication – The team has created an environment that makes it safe for one another to express concerns, expectations, and desires. They listen to each other, they acknowledge one another for their contributions and they are sensitive to each other's needs to be effective on the field. You can see it on the field and hear it in the post-game interviews.

There is no set recipe or blueprint to creating a shared vision. Each organization's process will reflect it's own individuality. However, when setting this ball in motion, start with your employees and developing their personal visions, then determine and consider the company's core values and purpose (chapter 1), set benchmarks to mark progress, and lastly remind everyone to be patient and keep perspective. Shared vision will not happen over night nor will it be easy, but you will reap the rewards in years to come.

DEVELOPING A SHARED VISION

1. What are the core values and purpose of your organization?
    a. Are these shared visions?

2. What significant thing/item/event helps create momentum in your organization?

3. As a leader what is one valuable thing you can do to catapult your organization?

4. What do you share with your team outside of company objectives and agenda?

5. Does your organization highlight shared success or individual success?
    a. How can you incorporate both?

6. As a leader, list when you've highlighted shared success?
    a. When have you highlighted individual success?

CHAPTER 3

CREATING A COLLECTIVIST GROUP

"Coming together is a beginning.
Keeping together is progress.
Working together is success."

-Henry Ford

If you want a team that sticks together and shares in your organization's vision and purpose, then you need to ensure that teamwork and team cohesion is present. The term cohesiveness is synonymous with 'togetherness' displayed by a team. Team cohesion can be defined as the force bringing group members closer together -- a group of people who work well together and enjoy doing so and that are committed to achieving common objectives and producing quality results.

While the concept of "team" has long been associated with athletic competition, the concept of "team" has since emerged into the business world and modeled for its ability to promote creativity, problem-solving, encourage decision making skills, and improve communication. The more success that is generated the better chance that group members will feel a greater sense of cohesion and satisfaction amongst one another. Coincidently, cohesion itself will also result in a greater sense of satisfaction.

How is cohesion and collectivism created?

Team cohesion can develop in a variety of ways. There is no exact recipe that you can reference, that will deliver team cohesion in a nicely wrapped gift box. Instead, you have to inspire, promote, and encourage your team to work together. Over time, encouraging participation from the ground floor will increase both the size and standard of the pool of in-house employees from which upper management can choose from to promote within the company.

What makes a team cohesive?

To create a close knit group you have to keep your group close together. Proximity is important when trying to create cohesion. Using college athletes as an example, coaches often times place entire teams in the same dorm building to encourage student-athletes to bond away from practice and the playing field. This same concept can be applied in the work world. Place team's and committee's desks near one another; close personal contact between team members facilitates interaction.

Find ways to differentiate your departments, committees, and teams. You can do this in a variety of ways, whether it is by painting each department a different color, or having them come up with team names; team members that perceive themselves as a unit and as different from others outside the crew will invest in their team. Get creative and have fun with this! Think about your group of friends and the reasons why you are friends in the first place. I bet part of the reason is because you have similar interests, attitudes, and aspirations while still maintaining your own identity. When putting teams together consider individual's attitudes, aspirations, commitments, and abilities. Those that are similar have an easier time creating synergy and cohesion. You don't want carbon copies of people all working together but a commonality that they can identify with will help with creating a more satisfying, efficient, and collective group.

For a volleyball team to be competitive and successful they have to be masters in group cohesion. They may set both team and individual goals but in a game setting everyone on the team is and has to be involved in the process. That is why it is important to place emphasis on the group's performances rather than individual performance. You can have the best outside hitter in the world but if the setter can't elevate the volleyball, the hitter's talents are irrelevant. Encourage your teams to learn about each other, understand each other's strengths and weaknesses, and to start talking about the process of their project or mission as they go along. During the process recognize progress and reward the team as a whole. If the team is cohesive there should never be only one individual that deserves recognition because everyone contributed to the desired outcome. For a volleyball team to win a point there is typically a bump, set, spike, and defense...six people are involved in the accumulation of one point, not to mention the bench support encouraging their performance. By placing emphasis on the group and not the individual you create teams that think about the 'We' instead of the 'Me.'

Lastly, focus on the structure of the team. It is very important that each team member understands, accepts, and enthusiastically undertakes their role in the team, as well as understands and conforms to team norms. I've played with teammates who were the most selfish people I have ever encountered and it was no doubt as to why we lost. Not only that but it was the coach who never promoted unity and allowed those things to infect our chemistry before and during its growing process. Individually we were a very strong team, but as a unit we were unable to put the talents together.

To help facilitate the development of team cohesion, ensure that the lines of communication are open between you, your upper management, and the members on the team. If open communication exists it becomes much easier to seek input when making decisions. Senior managers are a great tool to use to help implement change and to set realistic goals with the team that encourages their commitment.

Team cohesion is a vital part of the winning team formula. If the individual feels a sense of belonging and has committed themselves to the project and the project's goals, satisfaction and the motivation to carry on will be gained from the process of the combined effort. A leader who is able to come in and think these things through will be well received on making decisions.

CREATING A COLLECTIVIST GROUP

1. How much individual talent do you have?
   a. Is the individual talent uniquely different or is everyone similar?
   b. How does each person's talent fit in the organization?

2. Do your teams work cohesively together?
   a. Why or why not?
   b. If they don't, how can you improve this?

3. How can you leverage the strengths of one employee with the opportunities of another?

4. Do you do most of the creativity to improve the company or department?

5. What creative techniques can you come up with that will enhance the unity of your company and team members?

6. Do your team members have freedom to be creative and provide input in decision-making?
   a. Why or why not?
   b. If not, how can you improve this?

CHAPTER 4
SHARING YOUR LIGHT

"Lighthouses don't fire cannons to call attention to their shining - they just shine."

-Dwight L. Moody

We each have a plethora of gifts and talents within us. The challenge is recognizing what gifts you have and how to shine them onto others. To become a beacon of light you must first recognize your gifts. Start by thinking about what you DO have instead of what you DON'T have. Once you identify those blessings, your next step is to share your light by opening yourself up to others. Sharing the light of your personality is so critical to the improvement of your team's chemistry and community.

When you share your light you give off positive energy to those around you. That positive energy is warm, inviting, and draws people near. Sharing your light is how you stand out. Many people fall habit to waiting for something to happen, like winning the golden lottery ticket. They spend their lives hoping that something better will come along and light their fire. What they fail to realize is that they have already won the lottery. We have already been given everything we need to become successful and to make those around us successful too.

Your light is already on and some can see it but perhaps it is too dim for everyone to see it. You may sometimes dim your light as a way of not outshining others or to not threaten those you work with. It is time to stop playing small, and to start playing big. Start being that 10 that you are. When you let that inner light shine, and fully use your potential and power, you automatically empower others to do the same. We are all a 10 at something. Do you know what you are a 10 at? It could be as simple as being the best greeter for when customers come to your business, or it could be as large as a professional athlete, musician, or actor. The key to remember is that what you do well and better than the rest is your 10.

Sharing the light of your personality is so critical to the improvement of your team's chemistry and community. Sharing your light means that you give off positive energy to your teammates, creating a trust and willingness to go the distance for you. When they believe in you, they believe in your leadership. Sharing your light is how you stand out. Not that you are attempting to standout for personal satisfaction, but that you are standing out to promote the positive growth that your organization needs and deserves.

A lot of times our personal lives are completely different than our professional lives, but the Contagious Leader knows how to balance the two.

This person understands and has the ability to give 100% to both their professional life and their personal life; not short-changing any of their relationships. Take time and prioritize both your professional and personal life and figure out how you can be great at both. You will find that you are a much happier person when your life is balanced; as will be your family, friends and colleagues.

In addition to having balance in your life, you also want to make sure your team is balanced; that is why hiring a diverse group is very important. We live in the days of talent being vast. It's up to us to find the talent, mature it, and build a contagious team with that talent. Like you, each of your employees and team members are a 10 in something; one person might excel in data management, another could be a master in organizing, you probably have an excellent public speaker or a genius artist on your team. As a manager it is important that you connect teams as if you were doing a SWOT analysis.

How do their strengths impact the group?

How do their 'weaknesses' hinder the group?

What 'opportunities' does having this person on your team create?

What 'threats' could arise by adding this person to the team and is it worth it?

Now when you begin to individually assess your team you will already know who the alpha males or females are, who the snakes in suits are, and who prefers to keep the peace by not rocking the boat. When you can identify these trends and connect each person together it will make for beautiful chemistry.

In a previous job I had front line skills, I knew how to lead, I created prospects, I made high profile connections, I was focused on a vision, and I knew how to play the game, but I lacked the administrative skills to be the best. To overcome my lack of administrative skills, I partnered with others who did posses that talent. Together we complemented each other and appreciated one another's talent. Even today we join up on independent projects.

It's up to us to connect with our 10 inside of us and allow that talent to be a light to others. Some of us are a 10 in interpersonal communication, some of us excel in planning functions and events, or perhaps your talent lies in research and development. Regardless of what your 10 is, you have the opportunity to share your talents with everyone you come in contact with. Regardless of what position you hold, when you leave that position you should leave it better than how you originally found it. The only way you can do that is by sharing your 10, your gift, your passion, your talent!

Passion is something that grows as you grow. Sharing your excitement is equally important because your excitement and joy will be contagious to those in your direct realm of influence. Sharing your vigor for life and to the company's objective is also critical to the success and your light radiating. We are all passionate about something in a specific area, and that needs to be shared with others. This passion will evoke passion in others. It doesn't matter what they become passionate about. You first want them to experience the feeling of passion, and once they become energized by it, you then can start funneling that excitement in a productive direction that enhances the organization.

As a leader it is so important that we have an idea of the light we are sharing and how we are sharing it. As leaders we need to understand that our light will transform any room we go into. Transforming defined is to change the form or appearance of, to change the condition, nature, or function of. Contagious Leaders transform positively. For example, there are some leaders that receive warm reactions when they enter a room or arrive to work, and then there are other managers who go into a room and employees, teammates, coworkers cannot wait until they leave because of their poor attitude and negative aura.

Consider these points when you schedule your staff. When scheduling shifts, you have to schedule people who will complement one another. This is essentially critical in retail, sales, or customer service. Some employees are great at customer service and can win over every customer, but are horrible at bundling or up selling. Some sales guys sell at all cost and don't take time to assess the customer's basic needs; they just want the customer to buy. Therefore, you have to pair people up like this so you begin to allow their skills to complement each other. Will there be some friction early on yes, because there are two conflicting styles, but in the end, provided you are coaching them and allowing them to see your light, they will harness those out and begin to build a winning team. Encourage them to work together on a customer, by having one sales person greet and asses needs while the other sells to those needs and encourages additional sales. By using your positive energy you have manipulated this situation into something more positive, efficient, and productive – and that is what sharing your light is all about!

SHARING YOUR LIGHT

1. What are you a 10 at?

2. Does your passion exude throughout the organization?

3. Do your frustrations trump productivity?
   a. If so, how do you fix that?

4. How do you feel management / leadership transforms the environment?

5. Where do you relate in your ability to transform your corporate environment?
   a. Are you doing this positively or negatively? Be honest with yourself.

6. What things are you passionate about that make you stand out?
   a. How would sharing these things benefit your organization?

7. Does your company provide opportunities for personal development?

II
SHAPING THE MINDSET

CHAPTER 5
BEING CONTAGIOUS

"The essence of teaching is to make learning contagious, to have one idea spark another."

-Marvin Collins

Why in the world would somebody want to be contagious? Being contagious is typically labeled bad and encourages people to avoid contact with you. Contagious indicates the spreading of a virus for example from one person to another simply by being exposed to another's germs (i.e. sneezing). But the word 'contagious' can also be associated with many positive things, we've all experienced the contagious effects of a good belly laugh. One person tells a very funny joke and has the entire room in stitches. Like laughter and happiness, leadership is also contagious.

A leader who is contagious is an energized leader that acts as a catalyst – someone who gets people going. This person has the ability to raise the passion and enthusiasm of others so that they want to take action. They move others out of their comfort zone by believing in them and providing support to those that take risks. A contagious leader doesn't shy away from change but instead embraces it. They meet change and challenge with an open mind, tenacity, and optimism.

The role of leadership in business or in sports is indisputable. Great leaders create great teams and businesses. Mediocre leaders create mediocre teams and businesses. As a leader you must master the art of being contagious. We all know a contagious leader when we see one but are often unaware of what it is about that certain person that makes us want to be around them. We often say they have a certain je ne sais quoi. Fortunately, there are many great leaders that have mastered the art of being contagious that you as a young business person can look up to.

Consider former University of Michigan Football Coach Bo Schembechler, Bo was much more than a football coach. He was a contagious and great leader. He taught future CEOs, coaches, and military officers what value-driven leadership is all about.

Leadership is often confused with performance. Companies often label employees as "lead sales member" or "lead revenue driver." The difference between a "leader" and a "lead team member" is that the "lead team member" has the highest sales, services, or accomplishments, they do not necessarily actually lead people to be better as a "leader" would. Don't get me wrong I am all about results and accomplishments, but that's not what makes you a leader of people just a leader of numbers. A career based solely on the success of numbers will not get you promoted. You have to have a balance of individual success and the ability and experience of leading people to team success.

I have seen great athletes get promoted because they make touchdowns, baskets, and generate points. I have seen sales people get promoted because they consistently sell above their sales goal. I have also seen students occupy the seats of elite universities solely because their grades and test scores were the best. Now please don't get it twisted, individual success is vital to the success of the organization because each person brings something unique to the table. However, only generating impressive results is not the golden ticket to moving up the ranks through management.

A leader who wants to be contagious understands that, and the companies that promote them understand it as well. Leaders who are contagious understand that promotions represent change, not just personally, but collectively for the entire organization. A contagious leader recognizes that leadership requires the compassion to actively listen to your people, and then to have the courage to do what is right every time.

Being contagious allows you to infect others. One must be careful though, leaders with negative attitudes (whiners) infect others making the job more difficult for everyone. It is important to always be aware of your attitude when working with others. For example, when you encourage laughter, smiling, and enjoyment while on the job, your employees enjoy being at work. Google has the reputation as being one of the best places to work for because their working environment is so enjoyable. They encourage their team members to express themselves, they value inspiration from their employees, team members can bring their pets and children to work, meals are provided, and stress free and serenity rooms are on location for when busy days become overwhelming. From day one Googlers know that their managers and their company are rooting for them to succeed and that makes them want to come to work every day. Coming to work no longer feels like work to your team anymore, and many of their daily live stresses are taken care of for them so that they can focus on the task at hand. But not only does an environment like this help your team have a less stressful day but they also have a less stressful night. When they head home for the night they don't have to run around picking up children and pets, instead they can go home and have a nice meal with the family and look forward to another wonderful day at work. By setting up a contagious environment you are being a contagious leader.

Being contagious 24/7 is difficult; therefore you need to surround yourself with contagious people so that you can feed off them when you are feeling low or sluggish. You can find contagious people everywhere. Look amongst your current circle of friends, in your network of business colleagues, and start looking outside your network and create new relationships. Look for people who inspire you to be better, who empower others, and that always look to do the right thing every time.

With every relationship you have you should be focused on building greatness; greatness for yourself, for the other person, and for a better world. That is why those you surround yourself with are very important. Your relationships should be ones of construction not destruction. Constructive relationships lead to changes and advancement, while destructive relationships create wrecking and ruins. What type of relationships are you creating? Are u causing them to ruin or are u building empires?
Every day we wake up, we choose what attitude we are going to give the world, are you choosing to be positively contagious today?

BEING CONTAGIOUS

1. How contagious are you?
    a. Do people want to be around you?
    b. Why or why not?

2. If your employees had to say "my leader/coworker reflects_____." What would they put in that blank spot?
    a. Is that a positive or negative reflection?
    b. If it's negative, what would you prefer that adjective to be?
        i. How can you change that?

3. When was the last time you laughed with your coworkers?

4. Have you made the choice to promote positivity today in your organization?
   a. How?

5. What are you passionate about that could be contagious within your organization?

6. Can you think of someone in your organization that is contagious and how does that affect the organization?
   a. What can you learn from them and use in your leadership style?

7. How often do you coach someone in a positive manner when they make a mistake?
   a. Do you understand how and why the mistake happened or directly admonish the person?

CHAPTER 6

CELEBRATE VICTORIES ALONG THE WAY

"Celebrate more of what you want to see in life."

-Oprah

In our non-stop 24-7 crazy-busy world, it is all too easy to simply step over the win and get right back to the business at hand. As a manager, it is easy to get bogged down in those things that are not going well in the business, and to overlook or diminish the value of what is going well. When you are focused only on the grind, you often forget that your job can be much more satisfying if you only just took the time to enjoy you and your team's successes. I challenge you to not diminish your successes and victories, big or small. Celebrating these victories is important because it helps you keep perspective on why you are a leader in the company, what your broader goals are, and it gives you the chance to recognize others. Celebrating generates positive energy, builds your team and translates to more success.

5 Reasons to celebrate business wins:

- Celebrating the win reminds you that a good, focused goal works

- Celebrating boost morale and motivates your team to continue to deliver outstanding work

- Celebrating creates an opportunity to look at the big picture

- Celebrating allows you to create deeper relationships with your team by connecting in a way that is not just work-related

- Celebrating is joyful and makes everyone feel great – especially when it's the launch pad to a great weekend

Celebrations are something that can excite almost anyone. When you celebrate victories, it builds teams and teamwork. This is important because improving your team equates to improving your odds of growing your business revenue, morale, and customer's experiences all at the same time.

Enthusiasm is bred off of celebrating victories. When you have an enthusiastic team, you have enthusiastic customers. There are a handful of companies that do this well, Starbucks, Apple, and IKEA, just to name a few. Starbucks is not successful because of their coffee and its taste. They are successful because of the quality customer service that they give day in and day out. Customers enjoy their experience when they visit, whether it is a quick coffee stop on their way into work or long stay to study during college finals, the service is always friendly and consistent. When you have enthusiastic customers you generate income. The only way Starbucks can provide this type of service is by having happy employees who believe in the Starbucks brand.

The product doesn't even have to be amazing, but because of the enthusiasm and the positive feelings attached to it, people are more willing to buy it. Consider two ice cream shops on the same street. Both shops sell your favorite chocolate chip cookie dough (shop number two is known for having a creamier ice cream) for the same price per scoop. In shop number one, there is a waitress who welcomes you with a warm smile and treats you as if you were a guest in her own home. Shop number two has a punk kid scooping those creamy cones and is hardly ever at the register when you walk in. Even though you like the ice cream better at shop number 2, more than likely you will patron shop number one. Why? Because the customer service is great and the employee has enthusiasm for her job and the ice cream shop. Most are willing to have good ice cream and a great experience over great ice cream and a poor experience. When people are excited about something, they will find a way to use it, and share their experience with as many as possible.

How do you ensure that your employees are happy? To retain good employees and create an enthusiastic team you have to compensate them well, praise them for individual success as well as team success, and create relationships with your employees.

Enthusiasm spreads to your employees, coworkers, teammates, organizations, and families. This is good when your team needs to beef things up, and add some more work hours to the equation. The key to having a quality victory celebration is that it should be someone else's victory you are celebrating. No need to throw a party for yourself. This can come off as arrogant or self indulgent, but when you find ways to become a fan of someone else, and search for ways to become a cheerleader for others, then people will want to share more things with you. This will generate more opportunities for you to encourage, uplift, support, and congratulate their successes. The more successes they have as a team, the more growth you will see in your company. This will impact the bottom line in more ways than one. Finding ways to have a party with your organization that highlights the company and their new direction or new achievement is a great way to build momentum, credibility, and support. But make sure it's a team win, and not an individual win. There is a big difference between the two, and the direction you go in will make a big deal.

CELEBRATING VICTORIES ALONG THE WAY

1. Do you celebrate other's success?
    a. If so, how?
    b. If not, why not?

2. What was the smallest victory your organization celebrated?
    a. How did you or coworkers feel?

3. What was the largest victory your organization celebrated?
    a. How did this impact your organizations team chemistry?

4. Do you celebrate your own success?
    a. If so, how?

5. When you have an individual success how do you use it to increase or promote morale?
    a. If you haven't been in this situation, how would you handle this if the opportunity were given?

6. What are some victories, large or small, that your organization has experienced?
    a. Were these victories celebrated and how?

7. What reward system is in place to maintain productivity and morale?
    a. If a system is in place, does it work?
    b. Why or why not?

III
SHIFTING THE MENTALITY

CHAPTER 7
EMPOWERING YOUR TEAM TO COMMUNICATE

"I like to listen. I have learned a great deal from listening carefully. Most people never listen,"

-Ernest Hemmingway

I have seen many leaders who take the role of communication, take the role of supervisor, of clerk, of gatekeeper, of CEO, of VP of Marketing, Sales, etc. The key here is they take the role and they monopolize the role. They don't share the spotlight with their coworkers, teammates, or comrades. They are a one-man show, or I like to call it the Rambo Leader. They go on and on about how they are going to fight the war against customer service, or advertising sales, or public relations and when someone comes up to them and says, "hey lets go this way, I see a clearer path," they fight it because it's not their own personal agenda. This is a true sign of insecurities and weaknesses that the leader has. Some insecurities can make us over compensate in other areas and some weaknesses will become our strengths if we continue to work on them.

The reality is this, the best leaders know how to 'Empower Communication' amongst their teams. They know how to encourage and uplift their teams, while allowing them to communicate freely, because they understand that 'WE' is better than 'ME' any day.

Empowering teams allow them to be better equipped for the journey ahead. They have a superior level of cohesiveness because roles are defined and creativity is enhanced. They sense like they are a part of the big picture. I know some CEO's think this is a hard task; unsure how to reflect this on the entry-level floor. It's simple, you reflect it in the boardroom, your boardroom staff carries it over to their management team, and the process continues until it trickles down to the ground level. The next thing you know it impacts your customers. Your customers will begin to say, "Wow, this company listens to me and they heard my cry, or my pain, or my excitement and continue to adhere to it." Hewlett Packard has embraced this concept through their "I'm an HP and this was my idea" campaign. Their newest line of computers have been created and inspired by the ideas of their customers. When customers feel like they are being heard, they will look at your organization as an exciting outlet to express their ideas.

How do you allow your entry-level teams to be empowered? You allow the open door policy to be in effect.

You have seen open door policies before, where they say they are open, but when you go inside and express yourself, you don't get promoted; you're now a problem, or a complainer, or negative, etc. I've been on both ends of it. But when you do go inside to communicate your wishes, you also better have some options and/or alternatives. I do not believe people should bring problems to the table, unless they also have possible solutions. This way we are working together to work through the best possible solution collectively. This will impact the greater good.

Other ways you can 'Empower' your team, is to run an idea campaign and request through each department the ideas you need to generate for a better tag line, or concept, or easier way to complete certain processes. Understand this; entry level people know what's going on sometimes more than the people at the top. The reason is because they are in direct line with the customer and they execute the process. In my management career, the further I stepped back from the fire the more communication needed to take place. What I mean in reference to stepping back from the fire is that as an entry-level employee you're right there where it's HOT. You are right there where the customer sees you and you have to come up with solutions, be quick on your feet, and implement procedures on the spot, some of which needed to be done yesterday. As you go up that ladder you're not right there on the front line in the so-called "heat of the battle." Yes you are a part of the battle, but unless you go on that front line and monitor and connect with your team, there fire will burn out because you have not empowered them to communicate their frustrations, hang ups, concerns, etc. If you don't do this, chances are they will relay bad experiences to the customers they touch and bad news travels faster than good news. But when you are there with them and know them and they know you, and you show them they matter then it's a win-win for the organization.

When you empower your team to communicate they will become your allies, because they will freely be able to prevent and praise all in one. They will prevent problems, and they will praise your support. If you want a team to run through the wall for you, empower them to be able to communicate to you. I've seen this on both ends where some managers where dogmatic, and others were all about freedom. The key is finding the balance between being a micro-manager and being completely hands off.

How do you find that balance?

This balance must be established from the very beginning. When you first hire in a new employee you must ensure that you outline the expectations of the job, what it takes to be great in your organization, and how you will train that person in their new role. Once the expectations have been laid out you can follow these four steps:

1. Show Them
   Use yourself as an example of how a leader behaves. Demonstrate to them what you expect from them by performing it in your daily initiatives; practice what you preach.

2. Teach Them
   Not only do you need to demonstrate how to be a leader, but you also need to mentor them as to why you do the things you do and how it will benefit the organization.

3. Coach Them
   Your mentee now knows what being a leader looks like and why being one is important. The next step is showing them how to be a leader. During their daily assignments and interactions with customers and clients, observe how they interact and point out areas of greatness and areas that can be improved upon. Encourage them to get better everyday and find ways for both you and them to maximize on their talents. Remember, everyone is a 10 at something.

4. Hold them Accountable
   At this point there is a clear focus on the job expectations, what the employees strengths and weaknesses are, and how they will continue to improve. The last step is to hold them accountable for becoming better. By holding them accountable you are setting a standard. Accountability will keep them working hard and help them remain on task of becoming a contagious leader.

You cannot have accountability without going through steps one through three. Managers that jump straight to accountability are doing their employees a disservice. Employees appreciate having a clear picture and once you have laid out the groundwork you will not have to monitor them so closely. Training well at the beginning creates more competent and confident employees, and they are more likely to feel empowered and dedicated to your organization.

When you look at some of your companies that have best places to work status, the common theme is "we feel like we matter, and our decisions matter." When this is the case it allows growth to take place in so many layers of the company, because the next super star, or great idea, can be in the cubicle down the hall or next door. Empower them and they will rise to the top, and their idea will rise to the top with them as they begin to scratch the ears of others around. **Success breeds Success.** You've hired them because you believe they will be best for the company; now empower them to enrich the company and themselves.

EMPOWERING YOUR TEAM TO COMMUNICATE

1. Does your team communicate freely with management and leadership?

2. Does your organization have open lines of communications?

3. Do you give credit to your team members when credit is due?

4. Think of ways your organization could enhance the lines of communication (i.e. scheduled meetings, message boards).

5. Do you honestly ever consider an idea that comes from those in your organization?

CHAPTER 8
NURTURE YOUR INSTINCTS

"The leadership instinct you are born with is the backbone. You develop the funny bone and the wishbone that go with it."

-Elaine Agather

Great leaders learn how to use their gut. They understand that their gut will guide them and allow them to make the best choice for that tough decision. Decisions are always tough to make when you are focused on creating a contagious environment because you can't think only about yourself and how your decisions will affect your growth; you also have to think about the team and their dynamic.

When I was training sales people a lot of them already had a killer instinct to drive sales and make a profit, therefore my training wasn't geared towards motivation. Instead, I had to teach them that the "win and sell at all costs" mentality was not going to make them successful in the long run. Eventually, they were going to alienate themselves from the rest of the sales staff and cause a dysfunction in the team, which would in turn cause negative effects on the company and possibly their job. If I allowed this behavior to continue I would have lost my job or would have had to terminate them.

In the news recently, there have been concerns over performance enhancing drugs used by elite athletes. During the 2004 Olympics five weightlifters failed their drug test and where pulled out just before walking to their stand. Not only was this public humiliation for the athletes and their countries, but it was also a setback for the Olympics and for the International Weightlifting Federation. When you approach competition in an aggressive way such as cheating or knocking those in front of you down, simply because they are in your way, you will find that your success will not last for very long.

Therefore, I implemented a system that allows you to gauge how to make a complete decision based on limited information. The rules are simple, if you could check all three points off then it is a good decision.

1. Is it good for the customer?

2. Is it good for the company?

3. Is it good for you?

These factors may appear simple and not complex, and that's exactly what I wanted. I didn't want my sales team to have to continually come and ask me for input. I wanted them to be empowered to make decisions based on their instincts.

Not every sales person hired in is equipped with the instincts to make decisions on their own. Many of my employees needed to be molded into the successful sales person they are today. Too help nurture them; I would simulate a real life scenario/situation and ask them to consider the above three questions when making their decisions and choices. Once the decision or choice was made we would discuss the process they went through to make that final decision or choice. Eventually it would get to the point that they could make the right call quickly and without my assistance. Training your staff in this manner is a great way to set your employee and team up for success.

Training is not the only focus when creating a contagious environment and when deciding what is good for the team. How you handle employee negativity, employee concerns and conflict is also important. When employees confronted me, I could ask them to look at every angle and decide if their complaint, concern, or conflicts resolution would enhance the entire team, create a lifelong customer, and make you better? I once had a very green employee ask me if it was acceptable for them to sell a customer the less expensive product because the customer appeared to not have the means to purchase the higher product. First, I instantly thought of Julia Roberts in Pretty Woman when she went shopping on Rodeo Drive. She didn't look like the ideal customer but she did have the money. Quickly following that, I asked the employee if only showing the inexpensive product was good for the customer? To avoid making the mistake as the sales clerks did in Pretty Woman, my sales employee would be better off showing both the expensive and the inexpensive product to his customer. Not only will the customer now have an option but they will also develop trust for the salesman, thus generating more business for them and the company in the future. This is one way to nurture the instincts of your team to make tough calls. When you give them a mental checklist it allows them to make decisions without running to you. Some decisions can't take forever to make because they have to be made immediately.

Leaders get to this place by nurturing their God inspired intuition and instincts.....I like to call this your Sixth Sense. Yes we all have five senses.

Instinct is your sixth sense; that subtle voice in your ear that sends you simple instructions on which path to take. Do u listen to it? Or do u ignore it? Leaders understand that a lot of their most successful endeavors have come into fruition by making the best "Gut Call." As a leader you have to develop your sixth sense, but you also have to get others to nurture their sixth sense. You have to get them to the point where they can make those calls confidently because they have been equipped to do so. Think of your green employees as babies. If you left a baby to lay and didn't coax and guide them towards the mother to eat, they would starve. The same is true with your employees; you need to guide them in the direction that will make them successful.

Our instincts are important to survival, in business and in our everyday life. Our instincts clue us into when something is or isn't right, and when danger is around the corner. It often amazes me that so many people resist their initial instincts, when we were created and nurtured through our instincts. We often forget that our senses, reflexes and instincts all work together and depend on each other. They have allowed us to mature and grow in life. Consider your instinct to pain; if you put your hand on a hot stove, you don't have to think "Okay, that hurts. I should pull my hand back now." Your body goes on autopilot, jerking away, often before you can even say "Ouch!" The same type of natural response needs to happen in business and leadership.

I've noticed that as people grow older they begin to ignore their instincts. They begin to rely on conventional wisdom in making a lot of choices. There is a flaw in this tendency. Your instinct is your gut and when you ignore the boldness inside of you that knows what to do, how to do it, when to do it, and why to do it in a specific situation, you often fall short. Your instincts are a valuable component to be successful and understanding who you truly are.

How to develop a killer instinct:

- First off, be patient. Rome wasn't built in a day. Developing your instincts is going to take time.

- Observe and be vigilant. Be observant of your own life experiences, as well as others.

- Recognize patterns in human behavior. When you are able to understand why people do what they do, what greed does to people, and what lies are created to cover incompetence, then your instincts will start to sharpen.

- Learn from every conflict you face. Don't settle for solving the problem; use every situation to test your ability to recognize outcomes and opportunities. If you made a decision and the outcome wasn't what you wanted, look for what went wrong.

Your instincts hide the key to your true self. You probably knew you were going to marry your wife or husband immediately just through your instincts, but decided to wait (use conventional wisdom). Not saying that patience is bad, but your instincts told you to stick it out before you got to that place. Instincts tell you whom not to marry as well. (Smile)

NURTURING YOUR INSTINCTS

1. Do you trust your instincts as a leader?

2. How do your instincts help you to promote unity/community in your organization?

3. How do you nurture the instincts of your team to make tough or smart decisions when you're not available?

4. What do your instincts tell you?

5. Think of a time when you didn't follow your instincts, what was the outcome?

6. You're only as strong as your weakest team member; is everyone trained to think strategically?

CHAPTER 9
SKILLFULLY BEING BOLD

"The challenge of leadership is to be strong, but not rude;
be kind but not weak; be bold, but not bully;
be thoughtful, but not lazy; be humble, but not timid;
be proud, but not arrogant; have humor, but without folly."

-Jim Rohn

Having a team of individuals with impressive resumes and charismatic personalities does not mean your team will reach their maximum height. Athletic teams prove this statement true regularly with a deep bench and outstanding statistics, individually and collectively. During the 1999-2000 season, the Portland Trail Blazers stacked their roster with an impressive group of athletes, Damon Stoudamire, Steve Smith, Scottie Pippen, Rasheed Wallace, and Arvydas Sabonis, making them perhaps the deepest team in the league's history. They featured an outstanding starting lineup and their guys off the bench could have probably started for a few other teams in the league. Pippen, who helped the Chicago Bulls win six rings, was brought in to lead the Trail Blazers to their first National Championship. Ultimately something was missing because the team was defeated by the Los Angeles Lakers in the Conference Finals after blowing 15-point fourth quarter lead in Game 7 of the series. They had the resumes, leadership and statistics that proved to be the making of the next NBA Championship team, and yet they still fell short of perfection.

What makes a great team?

Great teams are tough. Great teams don't mind making tough calls. Great teams go down swinging. Great teams attempt that last minute shot or sale. Great teams are quick to address problems and obstacles.

The Portland Trail Blazers were tough, fought until the end, made buzzer shots; what were they missing? BOLDNESS.

Boldness is the opposite of being shy. A bold person is willing to risk shame or rejection in business and social settings. This person has a willingness to get things done, even despite risk; broadly synonymous with bravery. An excessively bold person could aggressively ask for money, or persistently push a person to fulfill a request or make a purchase. Boldness does not necessarily mean obnoxious, arrogant, or pushy; it is possible to be bold, while staying silent.

The great teams, coaches, and companies that stand out from their competitors are those that possess BOLDNESS. Every year CNN Money names the top 100 Best Companies to Work For, in 2010 the leader is the technology powerhouse SAS. SAS wasn't named as the best company just because they are successful and high revenue generating. They were named the top company to work for because they have bold practices and focused on their employees. With a 2% turnover rate they offer a laundry list of benefits – high quality childcare at a low price, 90% coverage of the health insurance premium, unlimited sick days, an on-site medical facility, a free fitness center and natatorium, a lending library, and a summer camp for children. Employees understand and believe that the company is making bold decisions with their well-being in mind and thus they are willing to be bold for SAS.

Companies and teams that produce subpar results often prove to be timid and lack guts. I've worked for timid leaders, or teddy bear leaders as I like to refer to them as, and it is frustrating to work under them because they are so focused on not making a mistake that instead they do nothing. Doing nothing on a daily basis creates no forward motion. Instead, by doing nothing you are actually pedaling backwards and creating a downward spiral. Employees need their manager to be present in meetings and willing to voice their opinion and concerns. If you as a leader do not fight for your team then who will? Your team knows if you are willing to fight for them, or if you're just protecting your own rear. Teams that do not trust their manager will not perform at its highest level because there is no synergy between you and them. Show one person you have their back and they may outperform and sell out to an all time high; do the opposite and they will do their own thing. Being timid doesn't get you promoted.

Business leaders don't appreciate a "Yes Man," but instead would prefer to have an intellectual conversation with somebody that has their own opinion. They want to see that you have a passion for the business and seek to challenge conventional thought. You will know that you are working under an insecure leader when they are unwilling to hear your suggestions and refuse to discuss futuristic ideas.

As a leader it is important that you be bold; quit being timid and afraid to go out in the deep end! When I was growing up, I saw a lot of people learn how to swim by just being thrown into the deep end. Not saying as leader to go out there and drown yourself by doing more than what your skill sets allow you to do, but sometimes you just have to step out on faith and go for it. Being bold means taking risks; not only taking risks but by taking strategic risks! Being calculated is good, but at some point you have to just step out there. I believe that boldness is a skill. You have to learn how to be bold and step out there versus being afraid and cautious. Boldness develops skills in you that keep you becoming a forerunner. I believe that boldness when you are younger is the same when you are older. When you're younger you have zero fear. Fear only stepped in when you realized and kept the opinions of others. Ignore them and keep moving forward. Nobody wants to follow a coward.

SKILLFULLY BEING BOLD

1. Are you a bold leader, teammate, or coworker?

2. Are you bold enough to show appreciation for your staff, coworkers, or teammates in tough situations?
   a. How do you do this?
   b. If not, why not?

3. Are you bold enough to disagree with your team and offer your dissenting opinion?
   a. How do you do this and not cause friction?
   b. If not, why not?

4. Are you bold enough to ignore the crowd and opinions of others so you can promote a new energy into your company?
   a. How do you do this?
   b. If not, why not?

5. If boldness is a skill, how can you develop yours?

6. Are those around you doing what is trendy, or are they forecasting well in order to take calculated risks?
   a. How do you know?

IV
SPREADING THE MESSAGE

CHAPTER 10
KNOW HOW TO WOW

"You are always looking for something that has the wow factor."

-Steve Violetta

to 'WOW' is an important focus for me in all my teachings. It ingredients that I have carried with me throughout my years in customer service, sales, marketing, coaching, sports etc. Knowing how to 'WOW' is such a critical component in providing a contagious experience. So I ask you before you read any further: do you know how to 'WOW'? Do you know how to give somebody a 'WOW' experience? 'Wowing' your customers, allies, partners, and management is a key element to getting that promotion. I'm sure you're asking what that looks like by now. It's very simple. You have to make such an impression that those you connect with say: "Wow, he's a genius"; "Wow, she's smart"; "Wow, he's articulate"; "Wow, this store is clean"; "Wow, this team's customer service is exceptional;" or the one I get a lot is "Wow, he's so good looking!" (Smile) The way to achieve this is to focus on excellence.

Excellence helps set the standards that provide a quality experience. When you're doing things with excellence other people will notice and catch onto it. Excellence defined, is exhibiting characteristics that are very good and, implicitly, and not achievable by all. The great thing about excellence from this definition is not everyone can achieve it. The 'Wow' factor allows you to showcase something that not everybody is able to accomplish. This factor alone separates you from your peers and competition because it positions you as a commodity and not everyone is capable to do what you are doing.

In relation to creating a culture that is contagious, you have to infect this factor into the threads of your company's DNA. You do this by ensuring that expectations are clear and precise in the infancy stages of your company and that these principals are followed by every level of the organization; starting with you as a leader and your management team, and onward to your coworker's management team. Once the expectations are clear, you have to implement them into your organization through training and teaching with a level of excellence.

Training your staff and leadership team is extremely essential to the fabric of developing an organization that knows how to 'Wow.' If you want to be the best, you have to train like the best. Athletes, whether professional or collegiate train day in and day out for that one shining moment. On February 4, 2007 Peyton Manning's passion and talent for the game, combined with hard work, dedicated training, and mental readiness soared him to victory as he led the Indianapolis Colts to a Super Bowl victory over the Chicago Bears. In addition to winning the Super Bowl, Manning was also named Most Valuable Player of the Game. Manning 'Wowed' the world with not only his NFL record breaking performances but also with his humble personality and dedication to regularly participating in charity events. Manning trains hard in the weight room, but also trains his mind and soul on a daily basis. His level of excellence on and off the field sets him apart from his teammates and other athletes.

Regardless of your profession, proper training is critical to success. Training is a fundamental place where some companies succeed at a high rate, and others fail at an even higher rate. Combining high-level training with coaching, implementation, and evaluations creates a 'Wowing' result that can catapult you to the next level. Just imagine what it looks when everybody on your sales force 'Wows' the customer. When you train your leadership staff to carry the 'Wow' factor on their chest and lead by example, you create a team that respects, admires, and desires to follow their supervisor.

'Wowing' is not just about appearance, and results; you 'Wow' with your integrity, character, and ethics, by providing a superior product, in presenting your best self, and by living by the values that are consistent with the values of the organization and that have a high morality clause. Being consistent in excellence is the key to 'Wowing' your team, and the cycling continuing throughout the organization and ultimately to the customer. Becoming someone who exudes this 24/7 is extremely difficult and you will want to throw in the towel some days, but it is important to continue to strive for perfection. Jesus is the only one who can perfectly 'Wow' me, but every day I model my behavior around his teachings. I say this to remind you that you will struggle and you will fall but if you continue to persevere and have the desire to be excellent and 'Wow' those around you, you will prosper and so will your company.

KNOW HOW TO WOW

1. Thinking about your team, what are the positives and negatives of your manager, coworkers, etc.?
   a. How can you build off of those positives?

n you change those negatives to be positives that help build
m and company?

3. What would your teammates say about you as a leader (both positive and negative)?

4. How can you use those strengths they see?

5. What can you do about your weaknesses that will help enhance how your team views you as a leader?

6. Are customers 'Wowed' by your team's quality to produce?
   a. If not, how can you be better?

7. What 'WOWS' you about the organization you work for?
   a. Why?

8. Is your organization meeting or exceeding expectations?
   a. How do you know?

CHAPTER 11
INSPIRE THE WORLD AROUND YOU

"Method is much, technique is much, but inspiration is even more."

-Benjamin Cardozo

I love being inspired, and I hope that living an inspired life and inspiring those around you appeals to you as well. Inspiration can come from a variety of sources. Sometimes it is as close at our circle of friends and family. Other times, inspiration comes from those we only know by name. Some of these people have invented products and concepts to revolutionize the world. Others give us insight on how we should live. Some have dazzled us with their genius and art. Some have conquered mountains while others have built business empires. We have been stunned by the athletic strength and endurance of ballers, gymnasts, and marathon runners. Others have liberated nations by gaining freedom for the people. Some have dedicated their lives to helping others. Some are great poets and authors while others have entertained us with their musical compositions. People like Mother Theresa, Gandhi, Martin Luther King, Jr., Bono, and Nelson Mandela have all been noted to have inspired the world and made a difference in the lives of thousands, and you can do the same.

How to be Inspirational

Great leaders inspire other because they understand the aspects of destiny, cause, and calling. They understand their reason for being here on Earth, how they are going to act towards others and what they will do and how they will use their talents and gifts to encourage and serve others. Inspiring the world around you is a critical element to being contagious.

Gandhi's life was authentic, using how he lived his life as his message to others. Mother Teresa and Martin Luther King each had a vision so compelling that it attracted the passion of others.

What these leaders have in common is that they brought out the best in their followers through inspiration, rather than motivation. When you provide inspiration to people your vision spreads like wild fire and can create instant change. Inspiration and motivation are often used interchangeably. We hire motivational speakers to rev up the team and encourage them to shoot more baskets, run more miles, and lift more weights. We are so absorbed with perfecting our techniques that we feel compelled to drive and be driven in everything. We want to be numbers-driven, customer-driven, character-driven, fundamentally driven, market-driven, and results-driven. Often times these drivers also drive us to drink, gamble, or become depressed.

Inspiration is best communicated as a selfless act that doesn't benefit you, but instead is focused on the betterment for others. Inspiration emanates love and our willingness to do something for someone else; while motivation pushes fear and self-concern and is something we do to someone.

As a leader you want to create relationships that are not based on pushing people to do what's right, instead you want to create serving relationships with others that inspires their growth and makes your team, company, and community a better place. A servant-leader knows that others crave to be heard and to be engaged. They want to be involved in a genuine dialogue, free of debate and ridicule.

In October 2010, President Obama praised the Chilean mine rescue by saying "the unity and resolve" of the Chilean people have "inspired the world." So many people showed goodwill in this rescue – from the NASA team that helped design the escape vehicle, to American companies that manufactured and delivered parts of the rescue drill, to the American engineer who flew in from Afghanistan to operate the drill. These efforts were out of love for the human spirit and an answer to the question great leaders ask themselves every day, "How can I serve you?" Try asking yourself this question and I bet you will find multiple opportunities to serve others.

A great place to execute this question is at work when dealing with a problem. Shift the emphasis from you to them by asking them, 'How can I serve you?' You may catch them off-guard because a person with a problem is dealing from a state of frustration. However, after a moment of them wrapping their brain around your question, you will find that by asking how you can serve them, it removes all the baggage, and it gets to the root of the cause of the issue, and it puts the other person's needs ahead of yours. Depending on the situation, your response may be to offer to help financially, emotionally, or physically. At the conclusion of your conversation it will become evident that an emotional and spiritual burden is lifted from the employee, who can then shed the distraction of the problem and approach his or her work with renewed engagement and commitment, leading to greater effectiveness.

To lead you have to serve, and to serve you must decrease personal ambitions for the greater good. Look to inspire effectiveness by living each day authentically. Ensure that you have a clear sense of your life's purpose and commit to building soulful relationships with all those you interact with. You inspire people when you find ways (or stand) to serve people. By serving people you are an inspiration.

INSPIRE THE WORLD AROUND YOU

1. Who inspires you?
    a. Why?

2. How do you inspire yourself?

3. How do you inspire your team?
    a. Does it work? Why or why not?

4. What inspired you about the organization you work with/for?

5. Think of someone who inspired you in your organization and how that affected you.

6. How could you motivate and inspire others?

IV
SENDING THE LEADERS

CHAPTER 12
CORPORATE EVANGELISM

"Yesterday I dared to struggle. Today I dare to win."

-Bernadette Devlin

CHAPTER 12: CORPORATE EVANGELISM

Evangelism is defined as spreading your message zealously.

Everyone can be an evangelist; you just have to have a dream and an eagerness to sell it. You probably engage in evangelism everyday and don't even know it. Is the TV show, *The Apprentice* or *House* your favorite evening show? And do you talk about the show the morning after with your co-workers, talking about who got kicked off or how unexpected the ending was? When you speak out about something with passion and excitement, you are creating a buzz. Companies love consumers like you because you are their purest form of marketing and easily sell their dream to others. In this case you are selling a TV show. There is a good chance that another team member will over hear your conversation, become curious about the episode, and log online to watch it. Alas, a new viewer is born. The broadcast networks thank you for effortlessly evangelizing on their behalf.

Evangelism is the purest and naturalist form of selling because it is about selling what we are passionate about. When we express our inner joy and belief about something, others respond in a positive way because they recognize that you truly believe in what you are speaking about. We have to be the voice for our own cause because if you don't believe in it, who will?

There are multiple forms of evangelism. You can be a positive evangelist; a motivational evangelist; a leadership evangelist, a customer evangelist; the list goes on. Regardless of what type of evangelist you choose to be, you must always be screaming your evangelism for all to hear; you must scream your passion and create some buzz!

Your evangelism should always be a body of work; consistently changing and evolving. Before I dedicated my time to teaching emerging business leaders how to fundamentally be leaders, I had to learn the fundamentals myself. Through my experience as a college and professional athlete I learned team skills and as a sales associate I learned corporate fundamentals. As I moved up through the ranks I learned how to put those skills together, combined with other experiences, and learned how to lead. Through all this, the one thing that was consistent was my passion to excel and be great. My friends knew, my mentors knew, and my colleagues all knew my goals and where my passions lied. Everyone knew my goals and aspirations because I purposefully told them whenever I got the chance. By being a purpose driven evangelist, I connected others with my goals and passions and they in turn accepted the opportunities to help me reach those aspirations. I encourage you to start expressing your hopes and desires to those you come in contact with and find ways in which they can help you continue to move in the forward direction.

Evangelism can be uncomfortable for a number of reasons. The main one being the idea that you will be exposing your passion to someone you are unfamiliar with, someone who may reject your dreams and attempt to squash them. Unfortunately, that is reality and that can happen. You need to prepare yourself with how you will respond to that person and event. Not everyone is going to agree and encourage your ideas, but enough will if you show them how badly you want something and how hard you are willing to work for it. If you have ever held a job or been through a job interview before, then you have already had practice at expressing your desires, dreams, and aspirations. When you walked in that office and sat for an interview you put yourself in a vulnerable position to get shot down, but you did it anyways. Why, because the opportunities that could have possibly been available to you were much more important than being told 'no.'

Think about a current or past relationship, the two of you didn't begin dating because you happened to be in the same room together. You began dating because one or both of you desired to be with the other person and expressed your interest. You put yourself in a vulnerable position to get turned down and rejected, but again the positive outcome of being with that person outweighed the negative outcome of a broken heart. Had you not opened yourself up and asked for what you wanted you may not be sitting next to that pretty lady or handsome gentleman.

As a leader you have to highlight the causes and passions that your team will scream about. Let them know why you are passionate about the company and/or the product that you are selling. Show them how to get others excited. If your team is passionate about what your company is selling than customers will be too. Remember, evangelism is selling but it avoids the feeling of being pushy and numbers driven. Instead it converts people to change. Below is a grid that Guy Kawasaki created to show the difference between sales and evangelism. It is not enough to just want something, you have to believe in it and live it. When you are living it, people take notice and want to follow. Start living and screaming your passion...create some buzz!

Sales vs. Evangelism[5]

Concept	Traditional Sales	Evangelism
Motivation	Make Money	Make History
Philosophy	Sell to	Convert
Method	Inspire	Expose
Goal	Quota	Change the world
10 Percent	Commission	Tithing
When	8 a.m. – 5 p.m.	Anytime
Where	Clubhouse	Anywhere

CORPORATE EVANGELISM

1. Does the word 'evangelism' make you uncomfortable? Why or why not?

2. What are you passionate about?

3. Do others know about your passions and desires?
   a. If so, how are they helping you?
   b. Who else should know about your passions?
   c. If not, why haven't you told anyone?

4. Does your company/position energize you enough that you truly believe in what you are doing?
   a. Why or why not?

5. How would this spirit affect your organization?
   a. Is that a good thing or a bad thing?
   b. Why?

---

[5] Source: *Selling the Dream* by Guy Kawasaki

CHAPTER 13
LEAVING A LASTING LEGACY

"Actions are the seed of fate deeds grow into destiny."

-Harry S. Truman

The month of December is a big month for many people. It is a month of endings, celebrations, intense competition, championships, and new beginnings. Every year college roommates, friends and family watch their loved ones take their final steps as college students as they walk across that stage to accept their diploma. College football fans celebrate conference victories and anticipate bowl competition. On December 21, 2010, the University of Connecticut's women's basketball team celebrated as they created a new Division I NCAA Basketball record with a win streak of 89 straight games. What do all these events have in common? They all represent creating impact and a lasting impression. They represent the opportunity of leaving a legacy.

Webster defines legacy as "something transmitted by or received from an ancestor or predecessor or from the past." We all have learned from legacies left by others before us and whether we like it or not, we are creating our own legacy every second. People will remember us for who we are and what we do.

Many people fail to realize that their life is a mission, to leave their community and the lives of others better than how they found it when they first arrived. We only have a short time to make critical choices in our lives and to impact this Earth and those around us. Instead of focusing on their destiny and this mission, they get wrapped up in superficial things like economic status and material things, without noticing that a race is running around them and they are not a part of it. They are so busy, so rushed and focused on their own lives; they don't take time to measure their enormous losses and to realize how much ground they are losing.

Some people instinctively know that they need to be in the race. They recognize that there is a grand purpose – a purpose that can move them towards their life's destiny. When President Obama gave his State of the Union Address on January 28, 2010, he was setting the stage for his post as a leader of our country. His words seemed intended to quiet America's worries about today's pressing issues, urge the completion of programs, excite people to get involved with upcoming initiatives that will create his legacy, and create a climate of hope.

Anyone in a leadership role should be focused on reassuring their team and company about the future, create a positive environment, and encourage team members to get involved and fight for the cause. Consistently remind them that you want them to work with you, not for you. Movies like Gladiator, King Arthur, and Brave Heart, exemplify this to the 100th degree. The leaders have prepared their army for battle, evoked their trust, catapulted their energy and passion on winning the war, and then sent them out to battle with a final charge. That final charge is an example of a leader unleashing the greatest warrior in their team and encouraging them to fight like it's their last and most important fight. If teams worked like this on a regular basis, the outcomes would be amazing and fruitful.

You must not guide only through words, deeds, action, but also through character, integrity, and virtue. Great leaders, whether they lead entire organizations or a sports team, leave a legacy that surpasses them and fortifies their contribution to the growth and transformation of their group. How they leave their position has a lasting impact. As they close out their time with their team, leaders must channel their energy, hopes, and fears towards mentoring their successor and team they are leaving behind. It is your responsibility as a leader to help your employees' transition from their old roles into new roles, focusing on practices and passions. Practices are about transferring the knowledge, practices, and relationships that helped you develop your team behind to minimize disruptions and setbacks. It is important that as a leader you share the lessons you have learned that have been instrumental in your success with others. Introducing your mentees to key people in the business and helping them network will allow them to build effective relationships, catapulting them into successful leaders. Contagious leaders should only leave a team or organization with only compliments and positivity. Do not leave your anxieties and negative thoughts with colleagues and team mates; leave with dignity and class.

Implementing passion is critical to growing and maintaining a contagious culture; you have to build this into your culture. Focusing on passion is about managing your desires for the company or team. Leaders need to ensure that their team understands their vision but understand and accepts that once you leave their may be some revisions to the plan. Be in tune with your emotions and have someone you can talk to about those emotions – friend, family, or advisor. It is important to build in a transition plan to allow a constructive climate for those still involved in the team and for those just coming aboard. Remember, when you are leaving a team, whether it is because your term has ended or you have decided to move onto something else, to let them know that you are keen to the big picture and support the next generation of leaders. If these pieces are successfully addressed, it is more likely that your vision, influence, and a positive legacy will survive years after you have left.

Contagious leadership is all about cultivating a destiny and a heritage that is great and spreads like wild fire to those that experience your greatness. Someone else cannot create it for you, you must create it yourself. John Maxwell didn't want others to determine his legacy. He asked others, "What do you want people to say at your funeral?" What do want to be known as? What do you want your life sentence to be? He advocates that you choose what you want your legacy to be, pick your legacy now and work towards that choice every day.

The future contains the hope of what you want to achieve. But the current resides life in the moment and here is where true identity of character, virtue, strength, and victory lie. My roommates left a legacy of friendship, kindness, and love with me throughout our college years. The women of UConn's basketball team are leaving a legacy of excellence, competitiveness, and work ethic. What will your personal legacy be?

LEAVING A LASTING LEGACY

1. Have you determined your destiny?
   a. What does it look like?

2. Are you focused on your destiny?
   a. If not, what is distracting you?
   b. How can you minimize the distraction?

3. What kind of legacy will you leave behind?

4. Who do you know that has left a great legacy?
   a. What can you learn from this person?

5. What choices can you make today that will enhance your tomorrow?

EXECUTIVE SUMMARY

<u>Purpose:</u> Regardless of your Position you can set the tone of your group. Contagious Leadership will serve as a blue print to the professional and entrepreneur to start embracing there leadership potential. This book provides business leaders with the tools they need to apply to careers right now. Contagious Leadership will also serve as guidance and a resource for the reader too reflect on their current position and how they contribute to the overall team, design a leadership style, and establish a game plan.

<u>Vision:</u> Contagious Leadership will inspire readers to stand up and start actively leading, regardless of position, by engaging, inspiring, and encouraging those around them. Through this book, the reader will walk away with the understanding of how to move towards creating a contagious environment.

Within a year of publication, this book will affect the lives of professionals and serve as an inspiration. At the time of publication, I am traveling internationally conducting leadership seminars and workshops. As Contagious Leadership is placed in the hands of individuals, it will serve as a catalyst for readers to be effective in their life.

<u>Target Audience:</u> Entrepreneurs, Professionals & Coaches

<u>Chapter Summaries:</u>

Contagious Leadership is designed to give you the guidance and ingredients that are essential too having a contagious, infectious, and positive environment. Leadership is a common thread amongst the generations of today, and several outlets attempt to give practical guidance. When using these custom designed practical action steps within your organization, leaders will begin to emerge and your team will become more effective. Adopting these concepts will ultimately allow you and your emerging leaders to evolve into their roles as managers and mentors. I chose the title Contagious Leadership because that's what I've always aimed to be as a leader, someone who can positively invoke change through my words, actions, and encouragement of others. Leading with the insight of providing a contagious environment is the preference of this book.

I. SHARING THE ROLES

Chapter 1
Crafting a Shared Purpose

Sharing is a form of teamwork that has to happen in order for a team to be effective. The 2004 Detroit Pistons proved that teamwork is the key to winning championships. Their camaraderie and ability to mesh as a unit catapulted them to win the 2004 NBA Championships. Had Chauncey Billups been the only one shooting the ball, perhaps the Lakers may have won another title. Instead, all five players on the floor worked towards each other's strengths and assisted in each other's weaknesses, allowing them to create a powerful offense and defense that was unstoppable. A shared purpose allows your team to be involved in the process of establishing the best concepts for the team. When organizations allow everybody to be a part of establishing the purpose, it allows for there to be one common theme and goal to be achieved. When there is a shared score, it doesn't matter if a player is on the bench or in the game, everyone is a part of the victory. People want to win; they want to experience the passion of playing the game and winning, and when you win as a team it is even sweeter. A shared purpose throughout your organization will allow your team to win and win together, making it a more positive and passionate environment to work in.

Chapter 2
Developing a Shared Vision

Creating a shared vision catapults your organization to another level. Most organizations share the company's vision with their employees by simply communicating it with their team; not realizing the actual strength and potential behind the seed they are planting. Organizations have the illusion that the entire team is involved in the development, process, and implementation of the company's vision, but in actuality the vision is casted onto employees by upper management, leaving employees with no sense of ownership or involvement. When a Leader can create a shared vision with their team in the infancy stages, employees are more likely to be less resistant and to buy-in at its roots. Having a clear, distinct vision generates commitment, excitement, and passion within a group. When employees bleed the company's mission, the climb to the top becomes so much more exciting and their efforts come into fruition.

Chapter 3
Creating a Collectivist Group

When people create things collectively they are committed to it. When an organization allows the team to create the purpose and vision collectively, a sense of trust and ownership is created; employees believe that they are a major contributor to the organization and feel obligated to perform at the highest standard. As your organization goes through the process of working together to grow and mature, they also equip themselves to effectively and efficiently handle any storms, setbacks, and or mishaps. Your organization will be equipped to wrestle through these experiences for the simple reason that the employees have a vested interest in the success and growth of your company.

Chapter 4
Sharing Your Light

Everybody has something that makes him or her unique; that separates them from others. Understanding the strengths of each individual and recognizing each of their roles is critical to the makeup of a team. A contagious leader understands this important factor and will strategically braid in each unique skill to impact the overall organization. When you share your unique self with the organization or team you add value to the operation. Stressing the importance of sharing your light will highlight your organization's overall value. Keep in mind that we shine brighter together when we shine by ourselves.

II. SHAPING THE MINDSET

Chapter 5
Being Contagious

Simply having results is not enough to get you promoted, nor does it create a following or drum up a group of lifelong supporters. Having the reputation of being a leader takes more than creating results in the field. You have to be contagious for people to take notice; you have to be able to replicate not only your results personally, but as a group. When you are contagious, you are able to impact the bottom line in your organization or group's performance. Through your example, people will begin to emulate your steps towards success and mimic your mannerisms in hopes to be great. Results get people to notice you, but being contagious motivates them too follow you. Nobody wants to follow someone that is negative or a complainer, but someone that is positive, upbeat and promotes constructive behavior…now that is someone they will follow.

Chapter 6
Celebrate Victories Along The Way

A team that celebrates together enjoys each other more and has more fun together. A team that finds ways to celebrate together will look for positive opportunities to continue the tradition. A winning tradition is hard to build, but when it is set in motion it creates a continuous flow of victories. Winning is contagious, as is losing. When you can create a winning organization it promotes positive expectations across the board. People begin to expect to win and look forward to celebrating those victories. When people begin thinking positively, they begin living like winners and making choices for the betterment of the team and for themselves. Even in the event of a lost, a winner will find ways to see the positive in the situation. When Lance Armstrong was going through his battle with cancer he paired up with Nike and created a slogan to "Live Strong." In an effort to create awareness and raise funds to help with cancer research, yellow bracelets were created. These yellow bracelets became a huge phenomenon and evolved into a clothing line. Even though Armstrong's cancer took him off his bike, it didn't kill his spirit and drive to be better. As a leader one of your priorities is to find opportunities to celebrate victories with your team. Not victories that you personally have, but things that everybody can be apart of. Team chemistry is built on shared victories.

III. SHIFTING THE MENTALITY

Chapter 7
Empowering Your Team to Communicate

How strong the communication is amongst management and team members is an important aspect to the overall impact of your organization. The thread of communication is essential in its efforts to connect your company's vision and purpose to the people who are to implement the concepts of it. Communication holds so much power because it affects the way information is transferred and perceived by the listener. When you empower your team to communicate their feelings, frustrations, hopes, wishes, and desires freely, you are then allowing them to share what's important to them. This may seem mundane and an inefficient way to use your time, but when you listen without constraints, your team will communicate more things too you as opportunities permit. Your team will begin to believe that their presence and opinions matter to the organization; that they make an impact in the daily business. Their ability to connect with the company creates a sense of empowerment and ownership. When you empower them to connect and communicate with you, you empower them to sell the company's product passionately.

Chapter 8
Nurturing Your Instincts

Instincts are a major player in your ability to be successful as a leader. They are even more important if you are to become a contagious leader. Your instincts are what allow you to be spontaneous while still being strategic. Spontaneity is an important aspect in living life and having fun, and it's also an important component in inducing the creative process. Your sixth sense is a vital component to making critical decisions. When making those critical decisions it is vital that you always keep the bottom line in mind. Whether the decision is an impulse buy or dealing with customer relations, it is important to be mindful of strategy and that sixth sense. Your sixth sense is part of your natural DNA and makeup; it's the part of us that lets us know who is our friend, foe, or enemy. Nurture your instincts. By nurturing your instincts you are also nurturing your success.

Chapter 9
Skillfully Being Bold

Some managers believe that being bold means being aggressive, taking no bull, and belittling their employees. The days of just bossing people around and making them do what you say are over. There is a new generation of leaders that are reasoning with people about what they would like for them to do and generating high profit and low turnover. When you are able to boldly communicate and assert yourself as a leader, then you put yourself into a different category. Your workers no longer fear you as a big bad wolf; instead they look to you for guidance and assurance. The ability to be able to showcase your bold decisions without offending people is a true skill. Anybody can say "No," but to be able to say no, explain why the decision you made is best for all parties involved, and have it make sense to your team members, is the ultimate feat. When you have made contagious decisions that impact the group, your team will be able to accept and respect those tough decisions that sometimes have to be made. They are less resistant to change when they believe you have their best interest and the company's best interest at heart.

IV. SPREADING THE MESSAGE

Chapter 10
Know How to 'Wow'

A WOW experience is a must have motivation piece for a contagious leadership team. Contagious leaders understand that for their environment to evoke the reputation they ultimately desire, they must provide a WOW experience. Through instruction, coaching, and examples, only the leader can cultivate the path to a WOW experience. Learning how to WOW is what will captivate your team, your customers, and anyone that is attracted to your brand. So how do you WOW someone? There are critical steps that I have outlined in this chapter to ensure that not only will you as a leader have these skills, but also that your team will have them, and ultimately your customers will receive them. Learn the steps on wowing all parties connected to you directly and indirectly will make your organization a first rated company. These skills you showcase will be consistently duplicated, thus separating you from the competition.

Chapter 11
Inspire The World Around You

Inspiration is an essential element for a contagious leader to maintain support from his team. Being able to inspire the world around you carries a lot of punch and to some it may seem like an unattainable task. However, it is the most critical component to the maintenance of a contagious environment. It is what is needed to withstand the endurance of the journey ahead. Inspiration drives success. There are many people out there craving for inspiration. As we have seen in this economic downturn, many people have lost their inspiration to find a job, to find happiness, to even get out of bed each day. When a Contagious Leader commits his legacy to the inspiration of all that follow him he doesn't leave his tenure unfulfilled. When I say, "Inspire the world around you," it does not mean you have to become Mother Teresa or Nelson Mandela, but take notice to the world that you are closely connected and related too and commit to enhancing it. I have outlined how to start this process and then matriculate into other areas. Start with your team, family, community and be the Mother Teresa there and it will fall into place.

V. SENDING THE LEADERS

Chapter 12
Corporate Evangelism

The words evangelism and corporate are not often words that go together. Similar to the church, successful establishments preach a specific vision and ask you to be committed to that goal. As a contagious leader how do you spread the company word without creating a cult like feeling? When you are a contagious leader it is up to you to create an evangelistic environment in your corporation. I'm not conveying that you create a religious ceremony and do hymns within your organization on a routine basis. What I am suggesting is that you create an environment that is passionate and displays a religious fervor to all that are involved. Most evangelists are passionate about their pursuits and causes, and this passion exudes to anybody that they connect with, even if it's only for a short moment. The passion established by a contagious leader will transcend the environment now and in the future. Show me a contagious following and I will show you a corporation that has the passion of an evangelical.

Chapter 13
Leaving a Lasting Legacy

Everyone knows the value of a first impression, but it's the last impression that may be the most important to your career. The leadership style you choose to invoke and the impact you make on a team or organization will leave a footprint of who you are and what you stood for. It is important that in business and in life we strive to leave our team, company, and community better than the way we found it. To do that you need to focus on being better every day and pushing others to be better. Only you can choose your destiny and what is said about you after you are gone. How will you choose to leave your team? How will you choose to leave your community?

At the beginning of each chapter is a quote that is intended to complement the upcoming lesson. At the end of each chapter is a Leadership Diagnostic, intended to provoke questions about the topic and how it relates to your situation and leadership style. It will also help you create action steps to becoming a more contagious leader.

ACKNOWLEDGEMENTS

I would like to thank my family, friends, and colleagues who have provided undying loyalty and dedication. Most importantly, thanks to God for everything I have and am.

ABOUT THE AUTHOR

Booking Info: Donte' Hill is available for corporate appearances, endorsements, corporate or private coaching, speaking, autograph signings, and private appointments.

Visit him: www.kcsportsconsulting.com

Facebook: Donte' Hill

http://www.facebook.com/pages/Contagious-Leadership-13/286484974697432

Twitter: http://twitter.com/#!/Donte_Hill

LinkedIn: http://www.linkedin.com/in/dontehill

Email: hilldonte@hotmail.com

(229) 860-0816

NOTES

NOTES

NOTES

Made in the USA
Lexington, KY
22 November 2011